Gifted and Talented Females Speak Out on Parental Influences and Achievement!

Mary E. Henderson

Hamilton Books
A member of
The Rowman & Littlefield Publishing Group
Lanham • Boulder • New York • Toronto • Oxford

Library of Congress Control Number: 2005932384

ISBN: 978-0-7618-3271-3

"A dialectical thought, as ephemeral as it may be, connects us all, one to another, in a moment of creative endeavor." ----*Mary E. Henderson*

Contents

Acknowledgments

This book is dedicated to my daughter, Glacéia; my late husband, Roy; my Fielding Graduate University mentors and alumni; my relatives from San Domingo, Maryland, and Anchorage, Alaska; and especially, the gifted and talented individuals that volunteered to be interviewed for this study.

. A "Participant Release/Informed Consent Agreement" for each interviewee is on record (Henderson, 2001).

Preface

The influence that parents have on their children as they grow rapidly from early childhood through adolescence to young adulthood is phenomenal. For some parents, the nurturing continues until their children have settled into a career that they enjoy or until they are able to support themselves.

Unfortunately, many parents have difficulties helping their gifted and talented daughters achieve successfully. Many gifted and talented females disappear, hide their gifts, or work in jobs that do not make use of their talent. This work is a study based on the perceptions of several gifted and talented females who conversed about how parental influences shaped their behavior and choices to produce achievement outcomes. As the females revealed their past and present history, their stories were inspiring, humorous, in some instances sad, and, above all, very educational.

Further, this work contributes to the literature in the areas of the role of parents, teens and the growing brain, the struggle of females to achieve equality, the underachieving gifted female, identifying gifted minority females, and reading for achievement. The scholarly literature, found in the first chapters of the book, refers to some of the problems encountered by gifted females to achieve academically, socially, and emotionally. These chapters also serve as a prologue to the stories of the gifted and talented females as they speak out candidly on parental influences and achievement. Other fields of study in which this work may be a valuable resource are achievement, parenting gifted children, counseling exceptional children, women's studies, and multiculturalism.

..This work is unique in that it can be identified with other works that have been written specifically about gifted and talented females in which the method of inquiry was a face-to-face interview, an exceptional method of gathering qualitative information. The stories of achievement by eight gifted females from cultural diverse backgrounds should serve to enhance parenting skills and help educators be more aware of the need to restructure their curriculum so as to not leave the gifted and talented female behind.

Introduction

Females from almost all backgrounds have begun to make definitive steps in the educational, economical, and political areas of our society. Completing a thorough search of the literature substantiated these steps in achievements; however, the most important evidence of these achievements was gathered in a realistic setting with several gifted and talented females that were interviewed about parental influences and achievements. The importance of their achievements became even more paramount when, according to our history, it was just about a century ago that this was not possible, for the role of the adult female was mostly one of working in the home tending to the needs of her husband and children. She was not expected to work outside of the home. If she did work outside of the home during the 1900s, she was more than likely employed in domestic services or another low paying job.

Although there have been significant advancements for females in the executive, administrative, and managerial category, there are still many areas that challenge her in these modern times. These areas are rooted in the basic equality of life and living. Economically, the female still lags behind the male. For example, the take-home pay females receive for working in the same occupation as their male counterparts is usually much less. As recently as 1991, women working full time had median annual earnings equal to only 69 percent of men's. In addition, women with college degrees had median annual earnings approximately $1,400 higher than those of men with high school degrees (Thornborrow and Sheldon, 2004). Unfortunately, this circumstance presents a problem for females long before they reach retirement age.

Thus, as females struggle to achieve their visions, life's internal and external forces place barriers in their paths. However, through great resilience, a substantial number of females rise again and again to knock down these

1

obstacles. Sqme rise up to become gifted and talented achievers guided by the influence of parents, community ties, environment, social relationships, educational opportunities, choice of careers, the economy, and political aspects. Though all of these influences have a direct connection to the level and quality of achievement, the most significant of these, in terms of early childhood, would have to be parental influences. Yet, how parents influence their children at an early age can make a major difference in their children's achievement outcome.

The subject of parental influences and gifted and talented females aroused my interest due to the nurture versus genetic concept of raising gifted and talented children to achieve. Some experts believe resolutely that genetics play the major role in determining the level of achievement of these children; whereas, the experts that believe in the nurturing concept hold that it is essential to nurture all children regardless of whether they have been identified as gifted, not gifted, or learning disabled. The preceding assertions remain controversial; however, the primary reason why this subject continued to engage my attention was due to the lack of achievement many females experience in our society, mainly because they hide their gifts and talents, they exhibit passive behavior, or they are not recognized by parents or educators as being gifted. Undoubtedly, too many of these females become our underachieving gifted students. They drop out of school, work in jobs far below their potential, experience depression, and lose their creativity forever. The long-range effect of this dilemma is the losses to society, for many gifted and talented children possess the potential to become great leaders.

There are still many unanswered questions about how best to parent gifted and talented female children. This work was created to answer as many of these questions as possible. Further, the contents of this work have been carefully outlined to offer parents, scholars, and educators tangible models for helping the gifted and talented female child achieve successfully in a world that presents many problems and challenges to her on a daily basis.

Chapter One

The Role of Parents

Raising a child is not an easy task. Most parents do not have any formal preparation for the role of parenting. They used their own parents as role models to raise their children, without realizing that they may not be using the best parenting skills. It has only been recently that parents have been taking courses in parenting and reading self-help books as a guide to perfect parenting skills.

The significance of parents in nurturing the abilities and potential of their children at an early age helps the children to be successful during adulthood. Consequently, sensitive nurturing is the most important aspect in the development of young talent, even more than genes. Further, high achievement in education and high career aspirations begin at home. For this reason, it is extremely important that the role of parents does not cease when children enter formal schooling. The parents must form a partnership with the school to nurture the child not only in learning but also in behavior modification. Campbell[1] (1995) believed that the main problem for parents involved maximizing their children's potential so that they could become high achievers in school and later in life. He explained, "Your parenting can make a difference . . . Parents that use the appropriate nurturing strategies promote optimal growth in their child's academic potential all through their school years."

Parenting a gifted and talented child is an even greater task, since the needs and characteristics of the child are usually different from other children. All children require nurturing from the time they are born and throughout their schooling, and the gifted child, especially the female, may require exceptional nurturing. One of the most prevalent problems that confront gifted girls is depression. Parents need to pay close attention to comments that their daughters make about themselves, such as, "I am tired of being a weirdo," or "I am tired of being different." Although intellectually gifted children have the potential to achieve the necessary emotional adjustment, it still remains that gifted children and their families may be at higher risk for facing certain kinds of stresses or psychological problems.

Another problem that adds to the dilemma of the gifted child is that some parents are in denial about whether or not their daughters are truly gifted although they have been given tests and teacher recommendations to enroll in the gifted program at their school. These parents must educate themselves to become familiar with the criteria that are used to identify a gifted child; otherwise, there is a strong possibility that the child will become an underachiever because he or she is misunderstood.

Just as some teenage females do not want to be identified as gifted because of peer pressure, some parents do not want to tell their friends that their child is gifted for the same reason and others. Raising a gifted child can be a very demanding job; if the child is exceptionally gifted, he or she can change his or her parents' life style (Webb, et.al,[2] 1994). The chapters on *Defining Gifted and Talented* and *Achievement* will help parents understand more about identifying a gifted and talented child.

MEASURING PARENTAL INFLUENCES ON ACHIEVEMENT

Can one measure precisely how parental influences help children achieve to their maximum capacity? A preponderant thought goes directly to this question with an immediate no answer because it would be mathematically and scientifically impossible to measure an enigmatic subject of this nature. If it were possible to measure the effects of parental influences on children, then parents would know exactly when they needed to give inspirational talks to encourage learning, study their child's learning ability to identify the best career for him or her, or determine when it is time to give a big hug to build self-esteem and boast the child's morale. Then who is in the best position to measure parental influences on achievement? Is it the child psychologist, the educator, the parent, the child, or all of these? One might say, of course, the educator can measure achievement in a specific category by using a test to evaluate learning. However, on the other hand, the parent or parent substitute has no such tool for measuring the long-term effects of their influence on their children to achieve and become successful adults. The child himself or herself must be the conduit of this information since there is no known person who can read minds. For example, a female foreign exchange student of African and Caucasian heritage had enrolled on a scholarship at a prestigious Ivy League school. She stated that she had encountered some problems with academics and with race relations. The parents thought their daughter was matriculating successfully to become an anthropologist when all of a sudden, she decide to stop school to become a Buddhist Nun.

Obviously, their child's idea of achieving in the academic sense was different from that of her parents, for in the Buddhist religion, she would be expected to meditate 19 hours a day, and work toward achieving self-perfection in a world away from everyday citizens. Moreover, most of her day would be spent in a world of silence. Thus, she had at a moment's notice decided to change her career field to begin leading a life of virtual silence, away from academia and the work force. This change of career field could not be called a disaster, especially if the change was a conscious effort on the child's part to solve an emotional problem. Nonetheless, did the parents of this gifted female student communicate with her frequently to see how she was achieving academically, socially, and emotionally, or did they leave it to chance, assuming that because of her high IQ she would succeed in the academic world without their nurturing? In this case, and without knowing all of the facts, it is logical to assume that the child needed to have communicated her feelings to her parents in a very trusting manner.

The fundamental component of parental influences is nurturing. This does not mean that the child should be overly protected but that the child must be the receiver of nurturing to the extent that the child is able to achieve successfully on his or her own. Rhodes[3] (1994), the former Director of the Program for the Exceptionally Gifted (PEG) at Mary Baldwin College, stated the following:

> The role of parents in "holding on" to their child is fulfilled when
> unconditional love and acceptance are communicated clearly, when
> the uniqueness of the child is affirmed by the parents, and finally,
> when the immediate needs of the child are freely met. (P.20)

This means that the parents must maintain a nurturing environment for as long as the need is paramount to help the child reach his or her maximum potential for learning.

The author of this work has established the following parental influences under the nurturing affect: High Expectation, Encouragement, Guidance, Support, and Role Model. Each influence has its own unique advantages for helping children achieve (See Model in Appendix).

High Expectation

Children will not achieve very much if very little is expected of them. Therefore, high expectation needs to be nurtured from an early age and continued throughout the three stages of growth: early childhood, adolescence, and young adulthood. The nurturing stage is extremely important to help the child gain confidence. By gaining confidence, the child has a better chance of accomplishing short and long term goals, succeeding in school, and gaining a clear vision to face the challenges that will confront him or her on a daily basis.

Super parents have high expectations for their children, and they seem to create gifted and talented children. What is the underlying cause of this phenomenon? It's a case of the parents managing their children's learning and behavior for as long as it is necessary to help them succeed on their own. These parents produce a plan for achieving the goal of having their child be an exemplary student. The plan includes instilling the necessary work habits and high expectations (Campbell, 1995). If you were one of several parents that came to "Back-to-School" night, to "Freshman Orientation," or to parent/teacher conferences, then you were in all probabilities a super parent. Super parents let their children's teachers know that they have high expectation for their children.

Encouragement

All children need to be motivated to help them meet the daily challenges of life, whether they are at home, at school, or at work. This motivation may come in the form of encouragement. Encouragement is one of the main links to sustain and promote motivation and high expectation.

Parents should take every opportunity to speak sincere expressions of hope, love, and assurance to their children. These overt expressions will foster positive behavior to help the children believe in their own ability to achieve as they grow toward young adulthood.

During his early childhood, the mother of a well-known musician encouraged him to practice the piano everyday although he was interested in playing football with his friends instead of practicing the piano. Later, her son became a famous composer; his songs are still popular today. His name is Burt Bacharach. Obviously, his mother had observed a great talent that needed to be encouraged.

Guidance

Parent substitutes, teachers, mentors, and ministers are in a unique position to guide children; however, parents are in the most unique position because they are nurturing the children under different circumstances and for a longer period of time. Customarily, children remain with their parents continuously until they go off to college or join the work force.

Guiding a child in the right direction requires skill. In the case of very young children, that guidance must be done by parents with the exemplary behavior of a manager, for no guidance or guidance without a real purpose, could signal the difference between a child making the right or wrong choice while dealing with a crucial decision. For instance, guidance can be as major as helping when a child selects a career, or as minor (or not so minor) as helping a child to realize the importance of being courteous. It has been stated that

90 per cent of the problems in the world today could be eliminated if people were courteous to one another.

Support

Support can come in a variety of forms: Four of the most recognized forms are financial support, moral support, spiritual support, and emotional support. Most parents are aware of at least two of these categories, financial and emotional support. The question is how much support is needed before the child uses his or her own effort to accomplish goals without depending on the parents. Although too much support has the possibility of enabling the child, too little support could cause the child to reach out to strangers for affection, money, or harmful drugs. Therefore, in order to secure a good future for their children, parents must utilize their managerial skills. They must teach their children from an early age to value their assets and show respect to others. They must also show their children how to problem solve or to handle a difficult situation without becoming overly emotional.

Emotional intelligence is extremely important as a child develops. It could mean the difference between a child with high ability floundering and one with modest ability succeeding. Emotional intelligence must be nurtured from early childhood throughout adulthood, as it has much to do with excellent mental health. Of course, many emotional problems can be curtailed when parents show unconditional love and affection to their children on a daily basis.

Role Model

As children grow more well read and social, they begin to look up to people that they consider to be heroes. They will take a profound liking for an individual to the point of emulating him or her. This individual may become a role model for the child. Furthermore, having a role model at an early age can be a positive asset for a child, especially if the role model has unquestionable moral values and a significant career.

Incidentally, some Presidents of the United States have spoken highly of their role models: President Bush spoke at President Reagan's funeral about how much he admired Reagan and how much he learned from him when they were both in office. Another example is how much President Clinton copied the political style of the late President Kennedy. Additionally, several athletes serve as role models for children who wish to be sports' stars. Likewise, examples can be cited from other vocations: astronaut Lt. Col. Eileen Collins, the first woman to command a NASA mission; Elizabeth Taylor, a well-known movie star; entertainers, Dolly Parton, Whitney Houston, the late Elvis Presley and Jimmy

Hendricks; and many other famous people are all role models for many individuals from the "Baby Boom" era and beyond. Today, many soldiers, male and female, serve as role models, especially during wartime.

Many children will choose their parents as their role model. This, of course, would be the ideal situation for an excellent parent/child relationship. The parents' values could easily be communicated to their child. Thus, the stage is set for a healthy parent/child relationship in the future.

SUMMARY

Parents must maintain a nurturing environment until the uniqueness of the child is affirmed and the immediate needs of the child are freely met. The five influences listed under the nurturing affect that must be managed by the parents on a daily basis are high expectation, encouragement, guidance, support, and role model. The parents must use these five influences to inspire their child to achieve to the best of his or her ability. Parents that are super parents manage their child's learning and behavior and produce gifted and talented children.

This chapter was created to set the framework for the forthcoming chapters. Another chapter that helped build the framework for this work is *Females: A Story From the Past*. Although the male has encountered many challenges in the past, his struggle to achieve is very different from the female's struggle. It was not until the year 1920 that the female had the right to vote, when the male, except for the African American male, did have that right. Even today, in our modern world, the female is still trying to "catch up."

As the reader peruses the chapters on *Staging an Interview With Gifted and Talented Females* and *Gifted and Talented Females Speak Out*, the reader must be open minded and recall the past and present history of the female to truly understand the objective of this work.

NOTES

1. James Reed Campbell, *Raising Your Child To Be Gifted: Successful Parents Speak!* (Cambridge, MA: Brookline Books, 1995), 2-45. Campbell's research team tested over 10,000 gifted children. He is credited with the word "Superparents."

2. James T. Webb, Elizabeth A. Meckstroth, and Stephanie S. Tolan, *Guiding the Gifted Child: A Practical Source for Parents and Teachers* (Scottsdale, AZ: Gifted Psychology Press, 1994), 53-54, 227-241.

3. Celeste Rhodes, "Modeling Interdependence: Productive Parenting for Gifted Adolescents," *Journal of Secondary Gifted Education* 5, no. 4 (1994): 19-26.

Chapter Two

The Brain:
A Complex and Remarkable Organ

THE SOURCE OF ONE'S GIFTS AND TALENTS

The brain, with its two hemispheres, is a highly complex network of neurons that communicate with one another. The neurons are the brain's basic unit of processing information. As messages are transmitted from the brain neurons to all the specific neurons, a complex process takes place that involves many thousands of neurons in different parts of the nervous system. Moreover, each hemisphere has a specific function. The lobes control or are involved in movement, planning, language expression, language interpretation, sensation, vision, hearing, long-term memory, and behavior. The brain's limbic system contains the hypothalamus, which regulates the emotions: feelings of relaxation, fear, aggression, and sexual arousal. The hippocampus and amygdala coordinate memory storage and recall. Yet, the brain can do nothing unless its neurotransmitters, such as norepinephrine, serotonin, and dopamine, are communicating effectively with other neurons. As one can see, the brain is a highly complex organ. Similarly, the source of one's gifts and talents is intricate and mysterious, and coherently, the most remarkable organ in the body, the brain, governs the source of one's gifts.

Teens and The Growing Brain

The brain grows on into the teenage years, contrary to the old assumption that the brain matured before one reached his or her teens. According to the National Institute of Mental Health (NIMH), in a recent discovery by researchers, the prefrontal cortex, a "higher-order brain center," does not fully develop until young adulthood. This knowledge paints a clear picture as to why some teenagers do not achieve successfully until long after the teen years. It also allows us to realize the dilemma that parents go through when trying to communicate with teenagers. Finally, this research lets us know that although the mechanisms for a gifted and talented person may be stored in the brain, this skill might not surface completely until the young adult years, and it is possible that the frustrations that these children feel may stem from the fact that the brain is still growing.

Motivation and Inheritance

Then, can one say for sure that if an individual is gifted or talented, he or she inherited that gift from the parents, or did that individual study long and hard to increase the synapses (the space between neurons) in order to facilitate a highly creative response? For example, Albert Einstein, listed as one of the world's greatest thinkers, was shy, dreamy, and kept to himself. During his elementary school years, he maintained only average grades and was not motivated by his teachers or parents; however, encouraged by his uncle, he taught himself analytic geometry and calculus. Today, although he is no longer living, he is well known for "Einstein's Theory of Relativity." It is possible that he inherited his genius for mathematical equations from his biological parents; yet, the fact remains that his uncle encouraged him to continue gaining knowledge on his own. Thus, in this example, the power of encouragement, one of the five parental influences, was confirmed. In addition, Einstein's success seemed to have stemmed directly from his desire to study hard over a long period of time. His self-motivation, ingenuity, and the inheritance of good genes served him well. All of these attributes were important components to be transmitted from one neuron to another to achieve a desired result.

Moreover, the old aphorism that one's intelligence is determined consummately by the inherit qualities he or she receives from the biological parents has been challenged by several experts in recent times. In actuality, the way in which the brain develops determines whether intelligence is a function of heredity (nature) or environment (nurture). More specifically, the way that the brain cells are stimulated to make connections is far more important than the number of brain cells. So, a rich intellectual environment would ensure one of the development of greater brain potential than would be expected (Rose, 1985). It has also been suggested that 96 percent of our mental potential lies unused. However, once we begin to understand how the brain's memory functions, the way is opened to use that unused potential, and the result is a measurable increase in intelligence, at whatever the age. With this knowledge in mind, every child has the potential to be gifted or even a genius. In this regard, this study refers to five components for one's gifts and talents to become an actuality: good genes, a rich environment, parental nurturing, brain maturation, and self-motivation.

Chapter Three

Defining Gifted and Talented

GIFTED AND TALENTED: RECENT DEFINITIONS

It is difficult to define exactly what is meant by gifted and talented, as there are a wide variety of definitions. Stankowski (1978) outlined five categories of definitions of gifts and talents: First are after-the-fact definitions. Those who are gifted have shown consistently outstanding achievements in a worthy sphere of human activity. Second, Intelligence Quotient (IQ) definitions set a numerical point, and individuals scoring above that point are classified as gifted. For example, many institutions use Terman's Stanford-Binet cutoff of 135. Third, percentage definitions set a fixed proportion of the school or district as gifted. Fourth, talent definitions refer to students who are outstanding in art, music, math, science, or other specific aesthetic or academic areas. Fifth, creativity definitions emphasize the significance of superior creative abilities as a main criterion of giftedness.

In the Marland Report (1972), the U.S. Office of Education defined gifted and talented by recognizing six major categories of gifted and talented children:

1. General intellectual ability
2. Specific academic aptitude
3. Creative or productive thinking
4. Leadership ability
5. Visual or performing arts
6. Psychomotor ability. (P.L. 95-561)

The children in these categories, by virtue of their outstanding abilities, are capable of high performance and have demonstrated achievement and/or potential in one or more of the areas listed above. Most programs for gifted children emphasize the first two categories, with a focus on intellectual ability and academic aptitude. They neglect the area of children with specific talents such as art or music, if the student lacks a measured high level of intelligence. Nevertheless, in 1978 and 1988, the U.S. Congress revised Marland's definition of gifted and talented. Presently, we have the Federal definition (P.L. 1000-297, Sec. 4103, 1988), which recognizes not only high general intelligence, but gifts in specific academic areas and in the arts. The definition also included creativity, leadership, and psychomotor gifts and talents.

Sternberg's triarchic theory (1997) of intellectual giftedness is a model that emphasizes the coordination of three abilities. Analytic giftedness, sometimes referred to as the componential subtheory, is academic talent measured by intelligence tests. Synthetic giftedness, the experiential subtheory, refers to creativity, insightfulness, and intuition. Practical giftedness, or contextual intelligence, successfully combines the application of analytic and/or synthetic abilities to pragmatic situations. The most important aspect of Sternberg's model of giftedness is that a single IQ number cannot represent intellectual giftedness.

Renzulli (1977) believes that giftedness consists of an interaction among three basic clusters of human traits. These clusters consist of above average general abilities, high levels of task commitment, and high levels of creativity. Incidentally, Renzulli's model is based on creatively productive persons who are primarily adults who have made valuable contributions to society.

In recent times, Gardner's (1985) theory of multiple intelligences has gained acceptance by the education community. Gardner believed that one person could excel in several categories. Seven of his multiple intelligences are as follows:

1. Linguistic intelligence is the intelligence of words. Examples of this type of intelligence are lawyers, journalists, editors, storytellers, and poets.
2. Logical-mathematical is the intelligence of numbers and logic. Examples are scientists, accountants, and computer programmers.
3. Musical intelligence denotes the ability to perceive, appreciate, and produce rhythms and melodies. Examples are concert pianist, composers, and vocalists.
4. Spatial intelligence involves thinking in pictures and images and having the ability to transform. Examples are architects, pilots, artists, and photographers.

5. Bodily kinesthetic is the intelligence of physical self. Examples are athletes, crafts people, mechanics, and surgeons.
6. Interpersonal intelligence is the ability to understand and work with other people. Examples are social directors, teachers, and administrators.
7. Intrapersonal is the intelligence of the inner self. Examples of this type of intelligence are novelists, therapists, and wise elders.

As one can observe, gifted and talented definitions vary. Regardless of the connotations or denotations, what endures in order for one to be considered gifted and talented is the knowledge and methods that support the choices the individual makes to solve complex problems. It does not make any difference whether these problems stem from the academic category or the performing arts division. Each has its own complexities. For example, an orchestra conductor has to be multi-talented while leading the musicians in order to achieve a superb performance. He or she has to be able to read and rearrange the score as needed, position his musicians for the best sound, anticipate problem areas during the performance, and deal with a myriad of other tasks while conducting the orchestra. This example serves to demonstrate not only a highly talented person but also a person with a superior creative ability. Many gifted and talented individuals become the outstanding leaders of our nation.

Chapter Four

Achievement

THE IMPORTANCE OF ACHIEVING

The motivation to achieve is developed; it is not inborn. Children must be given a secure environment in which to achieve, and while they are achieving, they must be involved in building self-esteem, academic success, and social relations.

Self-esteem

Self-esteem is necessary to help people lead productive lives. If one were to study the lives of prominent and successful people, they would discover that they had one or more parents, relatives, or teachers who believed in them as children. Recall the example in Chapter Two pertaining to Einstein when he was a child. Einstein's uncle believed in his talents and encouraged him to continue studying on his own.

To build self-esteem, positive feedback in the form of praise is required. If this positive feedback is not given, depression may be the outcome. Self-esteem is also related to mental health; the link between depression and low self-esteem is well established. If a child has low self-esteem, achievement is hampered. The result is poor academic and social competencies. Moreover, low self-esteem often contributes to a child's underachievement. However, one must be cautious with self-esteem. Too much self-esteem can be a problem. People with too much self-esteem tend to lose self-control, and do not have self-respect. The desired goal should be to have self-esteem and self-respect; they are both very important. In the case of self-esteem, if children are never praised for the good things that they do in our society, they will most likely lose the motivation to become productive citizens.

Self-esteem is one of the most valuable assets a parent can give a child (Harris, 1998). The foregoing statement is especially true for female children. The age-old notions that females are not as capable as males still exists in some segments of society; as a result, many girls have low self-esteem. They do not take the risks required to achieve; they believe that they are less capable than their male peers.

Self-esteem is built upon the experience of success, and with each success, self-esteem grows, and new goals can be taken on. Additionally, the role of parents involves shaping children's sense of themselves.

Academic Success

Academic success is extremely important for all children, due to their need to accomplish certain basic tasks as they develop from children to adults. The most important basic tasks of all human beings is to provide for themselves and their families, and in modern society, this·is most easily made possible by acquiring education and training. Maslow[1] (1971), a well-known philosopher, suggested that education is learning to grow, learning what to grow toward, learning what is good and bad, learning what is desirable and undesirable, and learning what to choose and what not to choose.

Literacy is another basic need for the achievement of academic success. Children need to begin achieving literacy at a very early age, as illiteracy among adults is a major problem in the United States. In 1985, Kozol claimed that 25 million American adults could not read the poison warnings on a can of pesticide, a letter from their child's teacher, or the front page of a daily newspaper. The number of illiterate adults could be higher at the present time due to the number of immigrants that have entered the United States during the last eighteen years. In almost all cases, the problem is that the immigrants have not learned to speak or write the English language although they have been in the country for a number of years. The problem of illiteracy among children is due to the lack of reading outside of school. Longitudinal studies have found that students watched television an average of 21.2 hours a week, but spent a mere 1.9 hours a week reading.

Education is a powerful tool for freedom. It helps children think about their own lives and pursue those goals that guarantee success.

Social Relations

Social relations play a very important role in helping children achieve successfully. Inherent in every child is the desire to belong and to feel loved; therefore, it is necessary for the child to develop social and emotional skills in order to assuage his or her relationship with society. Basically, the individual both creates and is created by the social universe of which he or she is a part. The two are inextricably interwoven, and any reference to one is an implication of the other (McLaren, 1994). Then, it is logical to assume that social influence affects academic achievement.

Motivation to achieve is the basic element to make people productive. It makes people improve things; it gives people a feeling of satisfaction with tasks well done. It develops self-respect, and gives people a feeling of responsibility for the future. Every child has some special abilities that can be recognized and valued. Therefore, by raising children to achieve, parents can help make the world a better place.

NOTES

1. Abraham Maslow, *The Farther Reaches of Human Nature*. (New York: Penguin Books, 1971), 40-51. He emphasized the "Behaviors Leading to Self-actualization."

Chapter Five

Females: A Story From The Past

THE RECORDED HISTORY

A nation has to know its past history in order to understand the present and to have hope for the future. The recorded history reveals the struggles that females had in order to achieve equality. The Women's Rights Movement, which started in Seneca Falls, New York in 1848, was the first giant step of a long and laborious fight for women to achieve equal rights. During this struggle, Elizabeth Cady Stanton, a gifted achiever and promoter of freedom, used the Declaration of Independence as a framework for writing what she titled a "Declaration of Sentiments." This document was the backdrop for the women's arguments. In the document, Stanton spoke about how men and women are created equal, that they are "Endowed by their Creator with certain Inalienable Rights; that among these are Life, Liberty, and the Pursuit of Happiness." In addition, Stanton enumerated areas of life where women were treated unjustly; for example, she wrote that women were not allowed to vote, married women had no property rights, husbands had legal power over and responsibility for their wives to the extent that they could imprison or beat them with impunity, and women had no means to gain an education (National Women's History Project, 1998).

Nevertheless, it was not until 1920 that women were given the right to vote. In 1923, Alice Paul, minority and the leader of the National Woman's Party, drafted the equal Rights Amendment for the United States Constitution. She argued that such a federal law would ensure that men and women would have equal rights throughout the United States. In 1964, the Civil Rights Act was passed, prohibiting employment discrimination on the basis of sex, race, religion, and national origin. In 1972, the Equal Rights Amendment (ERA) was passed, which stated, "Equality of rights under the law shall not be denied or abridged by the United States or by any state on account of sex." Because these Acts were passed, women gained more freedom and equality; however, the struggle was not over.

A Struggle to Achieve Equality in Contemporary Times

Women have struggled for equal treatment in the social, political, economical, and educational systems for over a century now. They have not been able to achieve to the best of their ability due to problems of inequality in the aforementioned systems. The American Association of University Women (AAUW) outlined these problems of inequality. Their public policy program delineated the need for the following: gender fairness, equity, and diversity in public education; equitable access and advancement in employment for women; vigorous enforcement of employment anti-discrimination statutes; fairness in compensation; programs that provide women with education, training, support for success in the work force, freedom from violence and fear in home schools, workplaces, and communities; and expansion of women's health rights.

Over the last 25 years of the century, the statistics reveal the following facts. Women are less likely than men to complete 4 years of college; they are much less likely to continue through higher levels of education and obtain professional degrees; at all educational levels, women have higher unemployment rates than men; women college graduates, on the average, earn less than men with an eighth-grade education; minority women earn less than any other group of workers (National Coalition of Advocates for Students, 1985). These difficulties are phenomenal, and in many respects, they have a direct correlation to the problems that were encountered by women who struggled to achieve equality two centuries ago.

Recent daily newspapers carried feature stories about the struggle of women endeavoring to achieve equality. A headline read: "Women win $54 million settlement . . . Morgan Stanley Brokerage forgoes trial to settle gender bias suit." This case had to do with settling claims of widespread sex discrimination on the job (The Associated Press, Tues., July 23, 2004). Another article from the Boston Globe contained the following: "Once again, the door closed against a female VP (Vice President of the United States) . . . ." It explained that Geraldine Ferraro wasn't expected to win the VP spot in 1984. However, it wasn't expected that our country would go 20 more years without a woman on the national ticket (Voice of the Time, Wed., July 7, 2004). From employment to politics, the struggle continues.

United States Supreme Court Justice Ruth Bader Ginsburg, winner of the 1999 AAUW Achievement Award, called for an end to divisions in American society. She was also the writer of the 1996 opinion opening the Virginia Military Institute to women. Former U.S. Labor Secretary Alexis Herman, while speaking at a business session, described efforts to close national gaps in skills, opportunities, and pay for women. She focused specifically on the pay received by women, which amounts to American women earning 75 cents for every dollar earned by men. She stated that this amount translates into a pension gap and a Social Security gap that hurts women long after they leave work. The foregoing comments illustrate to a high degree why it is important for females to take the necessary steps to achieve. Their future is at stake.

Chapter Six

The Dilemma of Gifted
and Talented Females

UNDERACHIEVING AND GIFTED

The words, "underachieving gifted student," seem to be contradictory or ambivalent. If an individual is gifted, how could he or she be underachieving? Nevertheless, during this decade, the word "underachievement" has been defined or described by several authors. Some of the descriptions follow: Underachievement is a significant gap between a student's potential and performance; underachievement is inadequate school performance by capable children; underachievement is academic performance that is significantly lower than predicted, based on some reliable evidence of learning potential; and underachievement is when smart kids turn away from education because their school problems are misunderstood. As one can observe from these descriptions, there is a lack of consensus concerning how best to define underachievement (Ford, 1993). Yet, it is a known fact that a number of children that have been identified as gifted are not performing according to the standards that have been cited in the literature.

Several factors may influence the underachievement of gifted students. Gifted children, according to parental reports, tend to be highly sensitive and compassionate. A study by Dabrowski (1972) indicated a linkage between giftedness and emotional endowment. That is, gifted children tend to have high degrees of emotional over excitability. These characteristics are misunderstood and are deemed neurotic by the psychological community. Other factors that influence underachievement of gifted students are poor self-esteem (discussed in an earlier chapter) and low academic and social self-concepts. This is especially true for middle-school females.

The middle grades can be a time of significant decline in self-esteem and academic achievement. Additionally, out-of-school factors probably play a role in the decline of self-esteem and academic achievement. As girls grow older, their observations of women's roles in society contribute to their changing opinions about what is expected of girls. If girls observe that women hold positions of less status than men in society, it may lead girls to infer that their role is less important than that of boys, or that they are inferior to boys. Davis and Rimm (1998) proposed that gender differences in underachievement may not be biological in origin, but culturally based. The pink or blue blanket, the colors used in the infant's nursery, and the expectations of docility and conformity for girls throughout early childhood initiate the gifted girl to the eventual underachieving role in society.

IDENTIFYING GIFTED MINORITY FEMALES

Today, gifted females continue to face conflicts when they are faced with resolving society's expectations of them as women and as gifted people. Many times, gifted girls have to deal with the biases of educators who are slow to identify them as bright; some counselors tend to channel them into traditional female careers. A similar dilemma exists for gifted minority children. While endeavoring to pursue their talents and interests, many gifted minority females are not recognized as being gifted. They get caught between two cultures, become vulnerable to peer pressure, and suffer from psychological consequences. Another important reason why many gifted minority children are not recognized as talented is because their gifts lie in areas that are celebrated by their ethnic group but not by Western society standards. For example, many minority gifted are talented in humor, dance, imagery, and creativity.

Webb, Meckstroth, and Tolan (1994) observed that gifted children include persons from all ethnic groups and lifestyles. They also emphasized that environment clearly has an impact on intelligence, and intelligence can be heightened through nurturance and hindered through neglect and abuse. Kerr (1994) explained how cultural aspects of an ethnic group may not be considered when identifying giftedness and giving support to minorities. For example, gifted Native American girls may be reluctant to show their abilities because they do not wish to stand out, which has been a cultural obligation for many years; African American girls continue to be blocked from achieving their goals due to the poverty of the inner cities, low expectations of academic performance, and difficulty in male-female relationships; and Asian American and Hispanic gifted girls often come from strongly traditional patriarchal families that, encourage traditional sex roles, which includes being a good mother and to be feminine.

THE IMPORTANCE OF IDENTIFYING GIFTED UNDERACHIEVERS

One might ask the question, "Why is it important to identify gifted under-achievers?" A fundamental answer is that there would be a loss of potential contribution to society from those individuals. Second, the underachievers would be susceptible to significant mental health and social problems, which become disturbing behavioral problems both at home and at school. Third, early identification would permit a better chance for reversing patterns of un-derachievement.

Another reason why it is very important to identify gifted females is that many gifted females will disappear. Noble (1988) suggested that a gifted person would not succeed against all odds, especially if she is female. The challenge of being both gifted and female is so great that without proper intervention by parents, teachers, and counselors, the majority of gifted females will continue to disappear. All too often, females develop negative self-perceptions due to the inability of people in society to recognize giftedness in females. Social pressures also contribute to the disappearance of gifted females, and almost all gifted females have had to hide their giftedness and behave in a passive manner in order to survive socially. Eventually, the result of their struggling leads them to underachievement, underemployment, dissatisfaction with life, depression, anxiety, illness, eating disorders, suicide, perfectionism and isolation.

Whitmore (1980) substantiated the fact that many children were not recognized as gifted underachievers in school, and later as they became adults, they discovered that they had superior intellectual abilities. Yet, their school records showed mediocre or poor academic performance. In view of this lack of discovery, society lost the potential contribution from those individuals.

Chapter Seven

Staging an Interview With Gifted and Talented Females

INTRODUCTION

The value of research is to uncover information that has been investigated previously, discover new information, analyze the information, and connect the dots. Discovering new information on a subject that is embodied in the human, educational, social, or economical systems is one of the most important goals that an author can achieve. The researcher deals directly with the well being of people, the solving of complex problems, and the construction of a new vision for the future. This study used qualitative methodology with an interview approach to collect information from gifted and talented female participants about how their parents influenced them to achieve.

During the interview, in addition to qualitative methodology, narrative inquiry, and a cultural-ecological perspective were suitable components for guiding the central question: How did parents or parent substitutes influence the achievement of eight gifted and talented females? In addition, the interviewer was able to listen to the participants narrate their past experiences, observe their behavior, and accumulate notes in order to share their stories.

How were the participants selected for the interview? Some of the participants were identified through a "Municipality Achievement Program for Women." Each year, the Municipality and a local petroleum corporation select several highly accomplished women and award them for their achievements. The selection was also the result of having knowledge of their talents, leadership position, and skills in the workplace and in the community. Recommendations were received from their colleagues. Additionally, the interviewer was cognizant of Sternberg's theory[1] that suggests that a gifted person has to be exceptionally good at something, and their accomplishments must be valued by society. Renzulli's[2] (1986) "Three Ring Model," which empha-sizes above-average ability, task commitment, and creativity was another method of identifying the gifted and talented individuals. Finally, Gardner's[3] (1985) multiple intelligences theory served as a major culminating point in the selection of most participants. He explained that intelligence is a cultur-ally defined and conditioned capability.

DEMOGRAPHICS

The participants came from diverse backgrounds, both geographically and culturally. All of the participants were female; their ages ranged from the early 20s to the mid-60s. They were all born in different states of the United States, including the Midwest, Northeast, Northwest, South, and West. Four participants were married, and four were single. Of the married participants, one had been married for 47 years, one for 40 years, one for 24 years, and one for 15 years. Three of the participants did not have children.

Other demographics that were significant to the study included the follow-ing: Seven participants had graduated from college; the degree is pending for the eighth participant. The colleges were located in the Midwest, Northeast, Northwest, and South. Some colleges were state colleges; others were identi-fied as prestigious universities. Two participants had Bachelor of Science de-grees, one had a Bachelor of Music, two had master's degrees, and two had doctor's degrees (J.D. and Ph.D.). Each participant had two or more family members who were either in college or had graduated from college. The par-ticipants had gained several job experiences, professional and non-profes-sional.

THE INTERVIEW PROCESS

During the interview process, the participants were requested to narrate theirs stories according to how their parents influenced them to achieve when they were in their early childhood, adolescence, and young adulthood. These three human development stages were outlined in the open-ended questions that were used as a guide during the interview process with all participants. The participants were asked the following questions:

1. Tell me about your achievements during early childhood, perhaps during elementary school age.
2. In what ways did your parents influence you to achieve?

3. How did you know, or who informed you that you had high potential for learning?
4. During middle school, senior high school, and college, how did your parents' guidance influence your accomplishments?
5. In what way did (do) your parents give you support during your early adult years?
6. What special ideas or recommendations (a quote, a suggestion, etc.) did (do) your parents give you that you recall from time to time, and how did (does) this advice influence your daily life?
7. What are some things that you value highly?
8. Is there anything else that you would like to share?

The place of the interview was either in the participant's office, a room in her home, or a room in the interviewer's home. The decorum of the settings was sufficiently pleasant to maximize the opportunity for uninterrupted, expressive dialogue between the interviewer and the interviewee. The interview was tape recorded with the participants' permission. To protect her rights of privacy, each participant's name was changed.

NOTES

1. Robert J. Sternberg, *The Triarchic Mind: A New Theory of Human Intelligence* (New York: Viking, 1988).

2. Joseph S. Renzulli, *The Three-ring Conception of Giftedness: A Developmental Model for Creative Productivity.* In R. J. Sternberg & J. E. Davidson (Eds.), *Conception of Giftedness* (Cambridge, MA: Cambridge University Press, 1986), 10.

3. Howard Gardner, *Frames of Mind: The Theory of Multiple Intelligences* (New York: Basic Books, 1985), 85-263.

Chapter Eight

Gifted and Talented Females Speak Out! Narratives on Parental Influences and Achievement

ANGEL HOPKINS

MUSICIAN AND ACTRESS

"Learning didn't only happen in the school environment, but it also happened in the home environment."

Angel Hopkins has a Bachelor of Music degree. She was born in the Northwest, and attended college in the Southeast and Northeast of the United States. She is 21 years of age; she is not married, and there are three people in her family. Her job experience consists of work as a paralegal, work in retail sales, performing music professionally, holding various internships, tutoring children, substitute teaching in the public schools, and recording music. The following accomplishments were listed: being selected to be in the 1993-1994 edition of *Who's Who Among American High School Students*, receiving dance and gymnastics awards, being accepted into a college program for The Exceptionally Gifted at age 15, getting Honor Roll awards in middle school and senior high school, being on the Dean's List in college, performing the lead role in the "Crazy For You" musical production at her university, winning performance awards for vocal renditions, and being called back for the Broadway Production of "The Lion King" while in college.

Angel shared her feelings about how her parents expected her to behave during her early childhood. She expressed that they expected her to perform to the best of her ability academically, and she was also expected to behave well socially. In response to the open-ended question about the ways in which her parents influenced her to achieve, Angel replied:

My mom gave me little mathematical activities and puzzles
and a variety of projects that would keep my mind stimulated
outside of the school atmosphere as well, which provided for
a more all-around education; that means that learning didn't
only happen in the school environment, but it also happened
in the home environment . . . they spoke to me as an adult; as
some people would say, "No baby talk." I realized that my
vocabulary had fewer restrictions than most children my age,
and I was able to express myself in a more open way. I guess
you could say that I was using vocabulary that people who
had gone to college would use, simply because I was raised to
think as an adult from an early age.

Angel continued by discussing the high expectations that her parents held for
her in middle school. She explained:

During middle school, it was pretty much the same as elementary
school. It was the development of support and making sure that
I achieved good grades, and in addition, they also tried to help out
emotionally just because I was going through physical changes,
becoming a young adult; so additionally, I would say, they made
me aware of my physical changes and how they would affect my
emotions and how I saw the world around me as I attended school
and tried to achieve learning.

Encouragement, the second parental influence in this study, was given in
the form of advice in many instances. According to Angel, she received encouragement from her parents after her gymnastics classes, singing engage-
ments, and dancing performances. She stated that they gave encouraging
words by examples of strength and perseverance. Another means of encouragement that was emphasized by Angel was that of receiving notes of encouragement from her parents when she was away at college. Angel gave the
following details:

I would say that my father always said, "If you believe it, then you
can achieve it." And he was a big stickler for having little notes all
around the house and all these encouraging statements that were positive
and made you want to believe. My mother was always a person that
was less spoken, but I would say she did it more in her actions. She
was the example of someone who was faithful to what they were
obligated to do and what they wanted to do. She was a person that
stuck to what she believed in, and so I would say one of the most
important things was an example, a living example that you could
look at to see what strength means and what courage means.

Angel spoke about her college experiences, and explained that her parents gave her little quotes on pieces of paper that they had copied with words for thought. She thought of it as a kind of food for growth with spiritual nuances. She stated, "I think part of that guidance with college was that they did allow me to go to college early and receive a more challenging education."

In reference to support from her parents, Angel responded:

> They always supported me. They took me to all my training sessions
> for ballet, gymnastics, tap, jazz, and for school programs, and that
> helped me to become a better performer in all of those areas. Emotionally,
> they supported me by attending my activities, my meets, and my
> performances at the Performing Arts Center.

Another example of support that was mentioned by Angel was that her parents helped her to establish herself in an apartment when she first moved to a large metropolitan city. This was financial support; however, she explained that they helped her emotionally too, by keeping constant contact and sending "care packages."

Angel explained that her role models were her mother, teachers, coaches, friends, friends of her parents, and professional artists. She added, "I would say also that people who took care of me at a young age: my babysitters, aunts, and cousins. Those are mainly the people that informed me that I had potential."

BEVERLY MCDONALD

OPERA SINGER AND VOICE TEACHER

"I can still hear my grandmother telling me that I would be successful, and I would never bring home any grade lower than a B."

Beverly McDonald was born in the Southeast. She graduated from a college in Tennessee, and took master classes in vocal music at a local university. She is a retired schoolteacher, a performing artist, and now teaches voice lessons at her studio. She has been married for 47 years, and there are six people in her family. Five people in her family have graduated from college. Beverly's accomplishments included the following: She was an elementary music specialist, she opened a music department at a local university, and she was an adjunct professor of voice and voice master classes. Other experiences included concert performances as a soloist with The Chamber Singers, Colorado Springs Chorale, several symphonies, performance with the Kennedy Center 1976 Bicentennial Chorus, and performing with the local opera company. She received the Freedom Foundation Award; Teacher of Excellence Award; *Who's Who Among American Women, 1968; Who's Who Among American High School Teachers, 1991;* and an Outstanding Service Award, 1993, from the local school district.

Beverly's grandparents had high expectations for her in academics and behavior during her early childhood. Beverly explained that she was the product of a divorce. Her mother died when she was 10 and her sister was 5 years old. They went to live with her maternal grandparents, and they and her mother's oldest sister became the constant influence in her life. Beverly shared her thoughts about her situation and the expectations from her guardians during the early stages of her life. While speaking about her grandparents, she proclaimed:

> They had reared their children, and now they were responsible
> for their grandchildren at age 61 and 66 . . . .Since I had no choices
> about anything, I did as I was told. I can still hear Mama Hughes
> (grandmother) telling me that I would be successful, and I would
> never bring home any grade lower than a "B." I believed her when
> she told me this.

In reference to her grandparents' expectations concerning her behavior, Beverly shared the following:

> I never had a free Saturday until I got married . . . I think I watched
> the university game, and I remember how I used to serve the Mint
> Juleps and the little bells to everybody who was going to the pre-game.
> They would come to this house for pre-game parties and then go on
> to the game, which, of course, we could not attend . . . and so they
> provided moral guidance. There was never a question about what
> a lady does . . . She (grandmother) taught me moral character,
> how to focus, and how to stick-to-it.

Besides the encouragement to bring home good grades, Beverly's grandparents gave her the following advice: Her grandfather advised her with this statement: "You can have ten cents in your pocket, and no one has to know it." Her grandmother said, "Carry yourself, young lady, as if you are a millionaire." Beverly conceded, "You were never loud. Children were to be seen and not heard, and that is what comes to mind."

Guidance was a part of Beverly's early days. She made reference to not having choices while she was growing up, inferring that her grandparents made choices for her. Beverly acknowledged that she used the "No Choices" method to help her children. This method was designed to not give the children a choice in the selection of their school courses until after they had entered college. Beverly selected her children's courses during senior high school, just as her grandparents had selected hers. Beverly affirmed that her children called back from college and thanked her for guiding them in their course selection while in high school.

Beverly expressed her feelings about her grandparents' support after her mother passed away unexpectedly when she was 10 years old. She intimated that a week after her mother's death, she and her grandparents were in court. She explained that the judge called her in and asked her with whom she wanted to live, her grandmother, or her father, and she decided to stay with her grandmother because she would have food.

In addition, Beverly explained that her grandparents worked to provide for two young children, Beverly and her sister. According to Beverly, her grandparents provided money for food and lodging after she entered college. Because she was gifted in music, she received a scholarship to attend a local college; therefore, she did not have to pay tuition.

On another occasion, her grandparents gave Beverly support by keeping her children for a short time while she was teaching in a location that was too far away to commute back and forth every day.

Beverly's role model was Miss Willis, who recognized her talent for music and gave her a role in the play, "Little Red Riding Hood," during elementary school. She declared, "From then on, music was a part of my life, thanks to Miss Willis." Other role models in Beverly's life were Miss Allen, her English teacher, who taught her to pronounce words correctly; Miss Cohen, who taught her to love poetry; Mr. Simmons, who taught her to love history; and Miss Dawson and Mr. Bartol, who taught her music and guided her during the adolescent years. Beverly continued to converse about her experience with her role models:

> I was listening to the Metropolitan Opera, which was broadcasted
> by Standard Oil. On Saturdays, we would go over to Mr. Bartol's
> house with a score. He would go to the White libraries and get the
> scores, and he taught us to read a score, so when I got to college,
> reading a score was not difficult.

Beverly also spoke about how much she admired her grandparents for helping her by taking care of her children while she sought employment as a teacher. She explained:

> They kept my children while I sought employment . . . I went to teach
> in Virginia; my husband was stationed in Michigan . . . I found a house
> to rent, and my children returned to me in September, so once again,
> my grandparents and aunt helped out . . . you know now it's a statistic
> as the number of grandparents who are rearing grandchildren. In those
> days, there was never any question. They did it all the time. It was just
> a part of our lifestyle, and not that of a statistic either.

Further, Beverly explained why her teachers were her role models. Her teachers were teaching in her elementary school and also in her Sunday school.

BERNADETTE DAVIS

SOCIAL WORKER, EDUCATOR, AND SENATOR

"My mother was a great role model . . . I don't know whether you know it or not, but I was adopted when I was 6 weeks old."

Bernadette attended the State University of Louisiana, and she has a Bachelor of Science degree. She has experience working as a nurse, a social worker, and a legislator. She has also been an officer on the local school district board of education. In 2001 she was elected to a seat in the State Senate. She has received numerous honors, one of which was being selected as an outstanding achiever by the local municipality and petroleum company.

Bernadette was born in the South, and has been married for 40 years. There are four people in her family, three of whom have graduated from college.

Speaking about her parents and their expectations of her during her early childhood and adolescence, Bernadette revealed how they were always there to assist her in learning.

> I was born in a small town; so as I remember what took place in
> elementary school for me is that it was quite a rewarding time,
> though I was going to a segregated school. I didn't know any
> difference, so even though we might not have had the best of
> supplies and materials, I had caring people surround me throughout
> my whole childhood. I had a mother and father that were really
> interested in their children . . . when I went to first grade, we did not
> have a kindergarten school where I went to school, but I remember
> even my dad used to help me with my ABC's and count with me
> and do all kinds of things, and my dad was not an educated man.

Bernadette observed that not only her parents but also the people in her small community were very influential in helping children achieve to the best of their ability. She articulated passionately about her experience at school.

> There were some people in our small town that were what you would
> consider being Special Education, and they didn't have any special
> program for them at that time, but they would let them sit in class. They
> could just do whatever they could do just to be there. They wouldn't

put them out. They just didn't have anybody to instruct and help them. In a sense, they were accepted. They had high expectations of us.

When Bernadette reached young adulthood, she was expected to go to college. She expounded on her parents' expectations.

They wanted me to go to a teachers' college, and I ended up going to a state university. We were told right from the beginning that they expected us to get all the education that we could, finish high school, and go off to college, and all three of us did.

Bernadette spoke about the encouragement she got from her mother. She explained that the encouragement she got from her mother was very advanced for her mother's age back then, in the sense that her mom was driving a car when most women did not even own one. She added that her mother was raised on a farm and made everything, including her clothes. According to Bernadette, her mom always used to say, "You can do anything that you want to do." She continued:

My parents are deceased, but many of the things that I learned there, that were taught to me, I passed that along to my children, and now they are raising their families, and I do believe that, "A family that prays together stays together."

There were specific guidelines that Bernadette was under while still living with her parents. She conversed about the details of the guidelines.

My mom and dad would come and visit me at college, and sometimes I would bring people home with me. They came with me, and they lived under the same guidelines I had to go under, and so if they came with me, they had to go to church that Sunday morning. And my mom was one of those people who didn't know what you could do past 12 o'clock a.m. They guided me all the way. Actually, I stayed up under that influence, and when I felt like I couldn't abide by that, because I had a lot of respect for my parents, then I knew it was time for me to move on.

Bernadette believed that she was blessed because she had a good background and caring people. She acknowledged that her parents and the community supported her academically and emotionally. The families in the community came to see her perform, and her dad always attended her performances. They were a close-knit family, Bernadette stated, and her dad and mom wanted their family to have whatever was needed.

When Bernadette resented her natural mother because she thought she gave her away, her adoptive mom gave her emotional support. Her adoptive mom explained to Bernadette that her natural mother was a teenager and could not keep her, and that she wanted the best for her. She also asked her not to resent her natural mother. Bernadette continued her conversation about her natural mother, and she explained, "She didn't have any more children, and so even though I didn't have a relationship with her, I did get to let her know her grandchildren, and so I feel good about that."

Bernadette's first grade elementary school teacher and her mother were her role models during her childhood. She stated that she admired her elementary school teacher because she took up individual time with her and the students in her class. Bernadette remarked, "There must not have been more than 12 or 13 of us in the room. We didn't know how blessed we really were."

In reference to her mother as a role model, Bernadette gave the following answer:

Now, what influenced me the most in my life? I guess it is my mom, because I really did look up to her. I admired her a lot. She was a beautician all her life. She loved her children, and she would do anything she could to make sure we got what we needed. She was a great role model . . . I don't know whether you know it or not, but I was adopted when I was 6 weeks old.

The interviewer was not aware that Bernadette had been adopted.

CATALINA CATHRON

ATTORNEY

"Her mother told her that there isn't anything you can't do if you set your mind to it."

Catalina was born in the Southern part of the United States. She is a graduate of Harvard University with a Doctor of Jurisprudence (JD) degree. Five people in her family have graduated from college. She has one child.

Her awards and special achievements consist of American Colleges Technological Scientific Olympics (ACTSO) at Carnegie Mellon, where she competed in the arts and sciences. She was the valedictorian in high school for 3 ½ years, and in law school, she received the Patricia Harris Scholarship. She also worked as an officer in the Minority Law Caucus.

During early childhood, Catalina's parents emphasized the importance of attending school. At home, her father would administer Intelligence Quotient (I.Q) tests to the children. Catalina spoke of her father's expectations of her:

> Well, in early childhood, my father was in a graduate program,
> much like your seasoned educators for the Civil Service. My
> sister and I were my father's test subjects for I.Q. tests and such.
> So, from my father's point of view, school is important, and what
> you know will ultimately be assessed.

Catalina's parents expected all three of their children to go to college. Her mother explained that it was not a matter of if you are going to college, it was just where. Whether it was a 2-year or 4-year school, it was sort of unspoken that the children were going to college. Catalina's mother advised her by stating, "You need to go, for the times are progressing, and you need to have that."

Not only did Catalina's mother and father encourage her to achieve, but also a family friend, a librarian, took an interest in her. The librarian encouraged Catalina to challenge herself with reading and to read many books. Catalina explained that it was more like a group effort. Her mother advised her to give it her best effort, but also be well rounded, and to do different activities. She also emphasized that, "There isn't anything you can't do if you set your mind to it."

Guidance was a major part of Catalina's family structure. While guiding Catalina in preparation for college, her mother asked her, "Do you want to go to an Ivy League school in the Northeast or a prestigious school in the Southwest." Catalina stated that the Ivy League school cost more than the prestigious school in the Southwest, so she selected the prestigious school; however, her mother said that she was going to the Ivy League school.

Catalina explained that even though she worked a little while in college, her parents carried the financial burden, so that gave her the idea that if you are going to go into debt, invest in yourself and your education.

Besides the monetary support for college tuition, Catalina also received emotional support from her parents, which, she stated was very helpful, since she was in a college so far from home. In high school, her mother was an advocate for her when she tried to enroll in the advanced French class. According to Catalina, the school administrator did not think she was prepared for the advanced class. Her mother told the administrator, "She can do this; let her go ahead." With her mother's support and assertiveness, Catalina made known that her mother showed her that you can and should stick up for yourself when you have the skills and believe in yourself.

Catalina's role models were her mother, a librarian, and a substitute teacher. She explained that her mother would give her and her siblings encouragement and general ideas as they were growing up. The librarian was a family friend and took an interest in Catalina. She helped her select challenging books to read. The substitute teacher became Catalina's role model because of a book that she recommended. Catalina recalled:

> In junior high school, there was a substitute teacher who noticed that I kept raising my hand to answer the questions. She came up to me after class and asked me if I had ever read *What Color is Your Parachute*. Since I had never read the book, I checked it out of the library, and discovered that it was a book about finding an appropriate career.

The substitute teacher gave her the idea that she could be thinking about careers, even in junior high school.

FRANCHESCA FRENCH

AUTHOR, TEACHER, AND MENTOR

"If I needed something, they were there, and they were there to talk to, and just to give advice."

Franchesca started college at age 17, graduated at the age of 19, and started teaching regular and special education classes at a local school district soon after graduation. She has a Ph.D. in Education and Mentoring.

During her early childhood, Franchesca attained several accomplishments: She won essay contests in elementary school, and trophies in swimming and bowling in high school. While teaching, she received grants in education awards, and won trips to educational conferences. Her most recent accomplishment is being author of children's books.

Franchesca conversed candidly about her parents and how they always had high expectations for her.

> I grew up in a family of four; I was the baby. We always had high expectations in our family for what we were to do. I was always on the honor roll. When I got my first "B" in fifth grade, I cried all the way home . . . "Oh, I got a B!" My parents just expected us to do well. Someone asked me once, "Well, did your parents praise you when you brought home your report card?" I said, "No." They expected you to do well, and so they said, "This is a great report card." It was like you did what you were expected to do, which was to get A's." So, it was the expectation, and I strived for that expectation.

Franchesca explained that a lot of what her parents did was kind of internal stuff, more than saying external things. She continued, "They expected me to go to college, they expected me and my siblings to excel, and it was expected by the community in which I grew up."

Franchesca's mom encouraged her by letting her know that she could do anything she wanted to do. She acknowledged that her dad never said it, but it was understood. Further, her mom taught her and her siblings not to care what people think, and in that context, Franchesca proclaimed, "You know, if you want to sing, sing. If you don't have a great voice and you are in church, who cares if you don't have a great voice. God wants you to sing."

During her high school days, Franchesca believed that her parents were very strict about the people with whom she spent time. She declared that she could not just go to someone's house and spend time, saying, "My parents wouldn't want me to go wandering, and so I found out I could take college courses instead."

Franchesca referred to her close-knit family when she was in her early childhood and adolescence stages, affirming the following: "You know, we watched TV, also, but we did things as a family."

Stating that she paid her own way through college, Franchesca made known that if she needed something, they were there, and they were there to talk to and just to give advice. When she spoke about her dad, Franchesca described him as "a strong, quiet man who was always there." She explained, "My dad never said, 'I love you', but you knew he loved you." .

Franchesca's role models were her siblings and her parents. She explained that during her early childhood days, she would follow her siblings around, and whatever they did, she would do. She also added that they did a lot of sports and won several trophies while competing in swimming and bowling. In reference to her parents, Franchesca admired their intelligence. She reminisced:

> My parents were very smart, themselves. My aunt went and did the Mensa, and she did the testing to do that. Now, I don't have any doubt that everybody in my family could all be a member of that, but we don't care. We know the intelligence, but we don't care to say, "Oh, I've got that." My parents are both Life Masters in bridge . . . incredible skill!

JOYCE JONES

❧ DIRECTOR OF HEALTH AND HUMAN SERVICES

"The expectation was always there that you are our child, and you're going to do well, and there's no question about that."

Joyce has a Bachelor of Science degree and a Master's degree in Public Administration. She was the Director of the Municipality Department of Health and Human Services for many years, and she has spent more than 30 years in local government management. Her accomplishments were recognized by the community and several organizations: She is the Chair of a local housing finance corporation, and she has received honors for her achievements from the Federation of Business and Professional Women during the National Business Women's Week 2000.

Although Joyce did not live with her biological parents, they still communicated with her frequently about their expectations for her future. Joyce expressed her thoughts on this subject:

> I really lived very little with them, but their influenced was
> always there. You know you've got to accomplish and do
> what you've set out to do, and you have a timeline to do it in,
> and so there wasn't a question, and I don't think I can ever recall
> asking, "But why?" . . . You know, because I lived in that era,
> "Because I told you so." And, that was good enough.

Later on during the conversation, when the talk centered on special ideas or recommendations given to her by her parents, Joyce explained their expectations:

> Well, not so much in my early years, but in later years, there
> was an expectation. The expectation was always there that you
> are our child, and you're going to do well, and there's no question
> about that, and I don't know that I have lived up to that expectation
> at all, but it was there. It was always, "You will do just fine."

Encouragement came from the educators at the schools that Joyce attended and from her colleagues. When Joyce was at a private school in the South, she and her classmates were nurtured by the professors and told that they were the leaders of tomorrow. During her adult years when she first started working in the government, Joyce had a mentor, the local mayor. She explained how he advised her to not be one of the boys because she would never be one of the boys . . . that they were nothing to aspire to be like, anyway. Joyce proclaimed, "That had more meaning than anything in my work life that anybody, including my parents, had ever said to me." She added, "It's very disgusting and frightening what some people are willing to do to achieve that higher level."

Joyce received guidance from her grandmother when she was in elementary school, from her parents when she was in high school and college, and from the dean when she was in college. When Joyce's grandmother walked to school with her everyday and stayed with her all day, she counted it as a very unique experience. When she was in college, her parents guided her with advice and love, and she was afraid to fail. Later, however, at a university, after spending her entire first semester playing pinochle, she was advised by her parents' and the official with the following words: "Ms. Jones, you have squandered more time than was useful, and now you've really got to get to it." Joyce was determined to finish college in 4 years, so she went to summer school.

Joyce's grandmother cared for her and spent time with her. In reference to her grandmother's devotion and love, Joyce replied,

> She was the person that my father said, "You are to take care of
> my child," and that's exactly what she understood. I was attached
> to her body and soul, so to speak, for all the years that she lived
> and the time that I lived in New York and went through most of
> my elementary school years.

As Joyce grew older, she explained that the support she received in her early adult years was confusing, but that she always received recognition and love from her parents, even though her parents had divorced, and both her mother and father had remarried. Joyce questioned why she did not have a stable home with her mom and dad; however, she believed that they were still very critical and important in supporting her.

The role models that were very important in Joyce's life were her grandmother and her mentor. Joyce affirmed that her grandparents in New York City raised her. She explained, "I don't think if I had an opportunity to have changed that that I would have wanted to, because it was whatever I am today; that's how I got here." Joyce continued:

> I am a grandmother's child. I moved to New York when I was
> a baby, and was raised by my grandparents. My grandmother took
> the responsibility of walking me to school every day. She stayed
> at the school all day, and sat on a little bench, and when school was
> out, we walked home together. It was really just the most unique
> experience, not that it was terribly appreciated all the time.

During Joyce's young adulthood, a mentor helped her enter into a government job. She revealed her admiration for her mentor:

> I had some tremendous teachers, and one of the best that I ever
> had was a local mayor, and he brought me into government. He
> taught me. I was in awe about what it took to be in a position in
> government that actually helped to set policy for how a city is
> governed.

Joyce's career in the government lasted for over 30 years, and during that time, she worked to accomplish many positive changes in government management.

KAREN PORTERFIELD

MANAGING PARTNER, PUBLIC ACCOUNTANT

"You know that 30 or 40 years ago, girls didn't do a lot of things that women do now, but my dad didn't care if I was a boy or girl, I could do anything."

Karen has a Bachelor of Science and an MBA degree. She is a public accountant. Her accomplishments are well known. She is the Managing Partner for a large accounting firm, where she supervises auditors and tax accountants. In addition, she is the first woman to become a Managing Partner in a Big Eight CPA Firm.

When Karen spoke about her early childhood, she remembered that she was always a really good student who always got straight A's. She recalled that she made the best or the second best grades in her class. After high school, Karen emphasized that it was her own drive that helped her to accomplish her goals. She shared the following comments:

> I don't think you go for your first 17 years in your life and have
> high values and expectations placed on you, without you either
> put them on yourself, or you don't. You either have your own drive,
> or you don't. That's my opinion. I would say that after high school,
> the drive and initiative to achieve came from me. They were proud
> of me and encouraging, but I think it was my doing.

Karen asserted that she was always encouraged by her parents to make good grades and to work very hard at school. She acknowledged that her mom was very proud of her achievements, but her dad was definitely more influential. Karen explained,

> My mom was very proud of my achievements, but she wasn't
> necessarily the one that was encouraging. I was the oldest child
> and had a very close relationship with my father. He was the one
> who always said I could do whatever I wanted to do. He was more
> of the coach . . . He was very encouraging, and he always intellectually
> challenged me.

Karen added that along with her dad, she had a very influential teacher who encouraged her even more than her dad. Her teacher would work long hours outside of school to keep up with the more challenging class that Karen had helped to formulate in elementary school.

When asked about a special quote or idea that was given to her by her parents, Karen replied, "You know that 30 or 40 years ago, girls didn't do a lot of things that women do now, but my dad didn't care if I was a boy or girl . . . I could do anything."

In terms of guidance, Karen recalled that her father had a lot of influence over helping her identify her skills when she was in college and in what a viable job would be. So, she counted this as an extremely helpful and encouraging time. Later, after entering the business world, Karen spoke of her mentor who guided her and who still works for the firm that is located in New York.

Karen conversed about the reasons why she is successful in her career. She revealed that she and three other partners, who were high in the firm, were sitting in a room one day listening to a client. During the interim, she recalled the following:

> I was the person who got the most information out of the client
> because I listened more than anybody else. Two of the partners
> were talking over each other all the time. The other partner, who
> is now retired, said to me, "You will be successful because you
> listen to people."

Karen's dad offered support in several ways; however, his coaching of Karen in academics and sports stood out. She expressed that he always intellectually challenged her, and that he would sit down, even when she was 12 or 13 years old and talk about politics and what was going on in the world. In addition, Karen explained that her dad did help a lot in terms of choice of careers. He talked to her about what she should do and what she should major in. She exclaimed,

> You know, he had a lot of influence over helping me identify where
> my skills were, what a viable job would be; so in terms of that process,
> he was extremely helpful and very encouraging; he didn't treat me like
> a child in terms of interacting and talking about ideas.

Karen's dad treated her as an adult while they were interacting and talking about ideas. For this and the other reasons mentioned before, her dad was one of her role models. The other role model was her elementary school teacher. Karen recalled her reasons for admiring her teacher:

> I remember one thing I did do when I was in sixth grade. I got my
> school to arrange an independent study class for a kid like me who
> was getting good grades and needed more challenges . . . I had a teacher
> who was very influential because she kind of went out of her way, and
> she tried to do something different for kids like me . . . She had to work
> outside long hours to keep up with us, and I would say she was the
> most influential one on my achievements in terms of earlier childhood.

MARTHA TAYLOR

POLITICIAN AND ASSEMBLYWOMAN

"They always told us that we were special kids, and we were very fortunate in that our teachers felt that way just as well."

Martha attended a university in Washington State; her degree is pending. She worked for her father's contracting business, for a daily newspaper, and for different advertising agencies. She also worked in the Governor's office, and later became an assemblywoman. Martha continues to work in the political field.

Martha's parents expected her and her siblings to be congenial to people and to have good manners. Her parents, in addition, stressed speaking correct or formal English and presenting herself always in a positive way. Martha proclaimed emphatically,

> I think my parents always encouraged me to do well. They were
> positive every day. They always told us that we were special kids.
> And later, throughout school, we were very fortunate in that our
> teachers felt that way just as well, and sort of encouraged us to excel
> and go beyond. We were very lucky.

Martha's mother was an elementary school teacher, and she was very interested in making education an important part of Martha's and her brother's life.

Encouragement from her parents helped Martha in many special ways. Her parents encouraged her to participate in a contest to paint a picture for the Winter Olympics that were held in Denver, Colorado, and she won a first place award for her picture. Martha added, "My parents always encourage me to achieve. They also encouraged me to present myself as someone who is relatively intelligent, and then to sell myself, which means to present myself in a positive and upbeat way."

Martha's mother always wanted Martha and her siblings to be kind to people, so she reminded them frequently to be courteous and to say, "Thank you" and "Please," and have manners at all times. Her dad reminded her to use correct English, especially while she was speaking on the telephone. Martha clarified her dad's ideas about why she should always be careful about speaking formal English:

> They (parents) were interested that we speak correct English
> because my father said if you pick up the phone and call someone,
> and they make sort of inferences about who you are on the phone,
> that means you don't get to the next step, so whether you have an

accent or not, it's important that we speak proper English, or come
off as someone who is relatively intelligent; otherwise, you are not
going to go anywhere. People make snap judgments about you from
the very beginning, and you want to avoid that as much as possible.

Incidentally, Martha worked in her dad's contracting business.

Martha spoke candidly about how her parents were very supportive of her
when she felt unwelcome at the University that she attended. Her parents told
her she could come home, and they provided a lot of emotional support. Another means of support for Martha was when her mother helped her pay her
bills while she looked for employment. Her mother requested her to try to get
something career-wise that she would enjoy.

Martha's role models were her parents, teachers, and a counselor. She recalled the information her parents gave her frequently: "They always told us
that we were special kids, and we were very fortunate in that our teachers felt
that way just as well."

Chapter Nine

Reading For Achievement

READING DURING THE EARLY YEARS

During the participants' conversations about their childhood, they revealed invaluable information about expectations, encouragement, guidance, support, and role models. However, other information unfolded about reading. Reading for achievement is one of the most purposeful activities a child can ever be involved in. Moreover, reading is the basis of all subjects. Reading was a very important part of the participants' daily activities during their early childhood.

The participants shared their feelings about reading during the interview.

Angel Hopkins

Angel spoke candidly about how she started reading at an early age. She explained, "I started reading books and writing stories over and over again. Later, I was tested and I was accepted into the Gifted Program at the age of seven."

Beverly McDonald

Beverly conversed about how she began to read during her early childhood. She reminisced,

> My grandparents were 60. So they were tired, and I don't remember
> love. I don't remember ever being told or held or made to feel secure.
> I lost myself, after my mother's death, in books. We had to walk to
> the old Carnegie Library. I lost and immersed myself in books, and
> I didn't have to think. I was told that that was my escape.

Bernadette Davis

Bernadette acknowledged the importance of learning how to read during her conversations:

> I just want to say how much I believe that learning is lifelong, and I
> try to instill this in my children and into my grandchildren. I've got
> two that do not read as much as I would like them to, but I know
> the key to anything is being able to read well and understand what
> you read and have a love for that.

Catalina Cathron

Catalina's school librarian encouraged her to read more challenging books. She stated, "The librarian pulled me aside one day and said, 'Well, do you always want to read these books?' Up until then, I chose books that I liked, but she encouraged me to challenge myself with reading."

Franchesca French

Franchesca commented on how reading influenced her during her early childhood:

> I remember for some reason, I was the youngest, but all the other
> brothers and sisters would sit by my dad's chair and read to him at
> night, like all of them, but for some reason, it never happened to me.
> I don't know whether he was done with it when I was old enough or
> whatever, but you saw all the reading they did.

Joyce Jones

Joyce's conversations about her school days revealed information that can be directly connected to the importance of being literate at an early age.

> My grandmother in New York died when I was in sixth grade, so
> the most traumatic experience of my life was leaving the New York
> School System and going to Oklahoma, where the work that I was
> doing in the second grade was what they were doing in the sixth grade.
> And, I was just so far ahead in terms of knowing how to research and
> just all those kinds of things that were part of the New York School
> System. I really didn't do very much the one year that I was there. I
> was kind of like a teacher's aide.

Later, during the course of the conversation, Joyce spoke about her experiences while she was enrolled in private school. She explained, "I was in private school for the seventh, eighth, and ninth grades, and the whole point of the school was nurturing and confidence and creating the leaders of tomorrow. Most of the students came from families who had major businesses in the South."

When Joyce left private school and went back to a public high school in Oklahoma, she added, " . . . I was way ahead in high school, so I skipped one year and finished high school when I was 16."

Karen Porterfield

Karen conversed about her advanced reading ability while referring to her accomplishments during elementary school and high school. During elementary school, Karen challenged the school system in order to introduce an independent study class. She was in the sixth grade at the time.

The conversation about her high school accomplishments affirmed that Karen never finished high school. She explained, "I left high school after my junior year and went to college because I had really good grades, and I was not challenged."

Martha Taylor

Her mother and her high school teacher advanced Martha's reading connection. She referred to her mother in an ardent manner:

> Well, my mother was a teacher. She taught elementary school for
> about 2 years. She was always interested in education and made sure
> it was important to my brother and me. At an early age, she would
> read stories to us.

In senior high school, Martha was placed in the Advanced Placement English class. The prerequisite for the class was excellent reading skills, and during the length of the course, she had to read several books, which was a requirement.

Chapter Ten

Discussion and Conclusion

DISCUSSION

This study explored the relationship of parental influences and nurturing to the achievement of gifted and talented females. All of the responses that were recorded and included in this book were from the participants' perspective. They were very enthusiastic about sharing information pertaining to their lives. They also gave accounts that revealed their personal experiences while achieving; they spoke about their family members, school, and the community where they had lived.

An analysis of the responses by the participants suggest that they started achieving at an early age and continued achieving as they moved through three stages of human development. Gardner[1] (1985) discussed his beliefs about intelligence and achievement at an early age. He suggested the following:

> A first point is that intelligences should not be assessed in the same ways at different ages. My own belief is that one could assess an individual's intellectual potentials quite early in life, perhaps even in infancy. At that time, intellectual strengths and weaknesses would emerge most readily if individuals were given the opportunity to learn to recognize certain patterns and were tested on their capacities to remember these from one day to the next.

It was evident that the parents or parent substitutes of these participants made plans for their daughters to become high achievers, not only during childhood, but for later in life. With the many references in the conversations about earning good grades and, "You will go to college," the concept that a profound connection between getting a good education and being successful in later life exists cannot be ignored.

High Expectations

A child's success starts with parent expectations, and high expectations need to be nurtured and supported by the parents. Although the participants were not queried specifically about expectations, each one either verbalized this directly or implied that their parents had high expectations of them. Further, the parents illustrated their high expectations by valuing education and letting their children know that they expected good grades and good behavior. Campbell (1995) explained that if little were expected, little would be achieved. The parents of the successful women in this study shared their expectations consistently, as referenced during the interviews.

Another significant observation during the interview was that high expectations was linked to careers. An example of this link was made when Karen's dad guided her in her selection of a career. In this particular instance, Karen's father helped her to identify where her skills were and what a viable job would be. Since a parent knows more about the world than the child does, the parent must blend his or her own expectations with those derived from the child, but the expectations must originate with the child's natural interests. Campbell (1995) referred to this as translating parental expectations.

Encouragement

Clearly, the participants were encouraged to achieve intellectually, socially, and emotionally. They responded to their parents' encouragement and advice by being motivated to achieve academically. Achievement was demonstrated when they brought home good grades, when they displayed self-confidence at a performance, when they worked to complete college, when they continued their education after completing 4 years of college, and when they shared their knowledge with others. In addition, throughout the narratives, the parents gave advice, in the form of adages, to their daughters. This advice may be seen as a means to build self-esteem and self-perception in their daughters. It also had a powerful connection to help build morale. All of these components were resourceful tools to motivate the participants to achieve to greater heights.

Guidance

Guidance can be interpreted as steering the child in the right direction. Kerr (1994) suggested that the problem with guiding females is that most parents underestimate their own abilities, and thereby, have trouble believing that their child may be gifted. Some parents are overheard saying, "Well, she's bright, but not gifted," as though gifted were the same as genius.

The parents and parent substitutes of this study took very seriously the role of guiding their gifted and talented daughters. They guided them as they made decisions about early entrance to college; they guided them as they moved to advanced classes; they guided them to select the most appropriate courses during high school; they guided them to select a college or career that would conform to their natural interests; they guided them in order to help them maintain proper behavior, self-respect, and confidence in their ability; and they guided them with love and mutual respect.

Support

Support was vital to create a secure environment for the participants to grow and be successful. In this context, the participants received academic, emotional, spiritual, and financial support from their parents, guardians, teachers, friends of the family, and the community. These individuals must have been very sensitive to the needs of all children; however, gifted girls require much more emotional support than most other females (Schmitz & Galbraith, 1985). The majority of the participants seemed to have been blessed with highly supportive and caring parents who gave them a safe and secure environment, which was conducive to their successful learning.

Role Models

Parents, grandparents, and teachers were recognized as role models during the course of the interview with the participants. Rimm et al.[2] (1999) wrote about role models for females, expressing the following point of view:

> Approximately half of the successful women identified with their
> mothers; a quarter identified with their fathers. Some women
> identified with their mothers early and then shifted that identification
> to their fathers or teachers as they matured. Some women identified
> with other people or no one. Parents were these women's most frequent
> role models.

Rimm (1995) explained that research clearly supports the importance of children's identification with good parent models as a family factor in high achievement, and the lack of that identification with good parent models as a family factor in low achievement. Fortunately, many gifted students learn to model their parents' values, and in the process, they present themselves in most situations as complete and not so dependent upon the opinions of peers, unlike most other adolescents (Rhodes, 1994).

Reading For Achievement

Obtaining excellent reading skills is an important requirement for all children. If a child is to have the opportunity to be successful in our society, then he or she must be literate, for excellent reading and writing skills are a prerequisite for all other subjects. Moreover, functional literacy is very vital for survival in our ever changing and challenging world. These skills are so important that they are taught and re-taught; reading specialists are consulted, literacy conferences are held, and reading experts emphasize which reading system should be used when a child first learns how to read. The participants in this study began reading at an early age.

Bingham and Stryker[3] (1995) explained how important it is to encourage children to read:

> People who don't read don't get very far in our society, and the
> situation is bad enough already. Today only 34.9 percent of
> Hispanics, 39.2 percent of African Americans, and 63.3 percent
> of White Americans can read proficiently by age thirteen. Young
> people with poor reading comprehension most often become our
> high school dropouts, and it's all downhill from there.

Parents should read to their children when they are young, and encourage them to read on their own. Parents must also promote a love of reading. This will ensure that they will read well in later years.

The method that is used when children first encounter the alphabet is extremely important for accelerated reading comprehension. Collins (1992) believed that the reason why her young students were able to read Shakespeare, Thoreau, Emerson, Tolstoy, and many other classical authors was due to using the phonetic approach to reading.

CONCLUSION

This study was unique to girls and women and to gifted and talented females. What does this mean? Summarily, it means that throughout this study, information has been presented which emphasized the need for parents and parent representatives to nurture female children, especially gifted female children, systematically from early childhood through young adulthood to ensure that they will produce successful achievement outcomes in their personal and professional life. If this has not been accomplished, many females will underachieve in their academics, they will succumb to peer pressure, and they will work in jobs that are way below their potential. Incidentally, all children should be nurtured equally; however, it is a known fact that many females do not receive the same quality nurturing as males; they receive less. This inequality between males and females dates back many years; however, females have begun to achieve remarkably well in a variety of career fields, including non-traditional jobs. Thus, they have begun to close the achievement gap.

The information that was gathered from the interview sessions with the participants was grounded in the following concepts: high expectations, encouragement, guidance, support, role modeling, and reading for achievement must be structured strategically and maintained systematically during the child's developmental stages. These stages are early childhood, adolescence, and early adulthood. The information also suggested that parental influences during the early years of development were extremely important factors in determining whether or not that child will be a successful achiever in her personal and professional life. If the structure and planning for the child's future is not in place, the child will most likely have severe problems on an emotional level, especially if the child is gifted and female and from a minority ethnic group.

Other important findings illustrated how the participants had internalized parental influences and strived to become high achievers. Those categories were self-motivation and their own personal values. Hence, one of the strongest areas of self-motivation was the desire by the participants to continue achieving in academics. The participants either skipped a grade level to enter college or advanced to a higher-level class within their high school, where they received college credit. Obviously, their parents and teachers had recognized their talents and had nurtured them to explore their talents.

Since the participants in this study were successful achievers and are still achieving presently, they are role models for other females. They have maintained their status as high achievers. Consequently, it is important to pass this information on to other parents so that they are able to use parental influences more effectively to help their daughters and sons achieve academically, socially, and emotionally. This is not an easy task for parents; therefore, this study was intended to not only discover information, but to conceptualize this information and to propose recommendations for practice.

NOTES

1. Howard Gardner, *Frames of Mind: The Theory of Multiple Intelligences.* (New York: Basic Books, 1985), 385.

2. Sylvia Rimm, Sara Rimm-Kaufman and Ilonna Rimm, *See Jane Win: The Rimm Report On How 1,000 Girls Became Successful Women* (New York: Crown Publishers, 1999), 16.

3. Mindy Bingham and Sandy Stryker, *Things Will Be Different For My Daughter* (New York: Penguin Books, 1995), 217.

Chapter Eleven

Recommendations for Practice

This study examined information about the parental influences that contributed to the achievement of gifted and talented females. The recommendations for practice are as follows:

1. Parents must have high expectations for their children from early childhood to early adulthood. If parents have high expectations, the child will have high expectations. In this same context, parents must dispel myths that undermine their child's expectations.
2. Parents need to establish continual support during the early years of their child's growth. This support should not be in the form of pressure or fear.
3. Parents must encourage their children to accept their giftedness. In addition, parents must teach their gifted daughters to empower themselves to reach their full potential.
4. Parents must guide their daughters to become leaders and to prepare themselves to compete in an increasingly technologically complex world.
5. Parents must act as role models. The most powerful influence parents have is through their example. By being an example, parents are modeling the behaviors they want their child to develop.
6. Parents must provide opportunities for their children to read at an early age. Additionally, they must help their children enjoy reading many books on different subjects, and encourage them to become lifelong readers.
7. Parents must help their daughters find their identity; for if not, they will be guided by peer pressure.
8. Parents may have to seek help for their daughters if they become underachievers, or if they become emotionally unstable. Several organizations

for females have been established today. An example is Operation SMART. This organization helps girls to get involved with math, science, and technology. Girls Incorporated, an organization dedicated to helping girls and young women overcome discrimination, serves as a vigorous advocate for girls, in that it develops their capacity to be self-sufficient and responsible citizens.

9. Parents must encourage their daughters to learn how to problem solve.

10. Parents must recognize that all children have gifts; that their gifts and talents may lie in one or more areas of intelligence but not necessarily in all areas of intelligence.

Chapter Twelve

Study Questions
and Suggested Readings

CHAPTER ONE   THE ROLE OF PARENTS

Study Questions

1. What is one of the primary reasons why parents encounter difficulties when they try to help their children achieve?
2. Given that each child is unique, why is parenting gifted and talented female children considered to be more difficult than parenting children that are not considered to be gifted?
3. What are the five most important parental influences needed to help children achieve to their full potential?
4. How is each influence unique, and how do they enhance one another?
5. What are the fundamental components that drive parental influences?
6. Showing your child that you love him or her is a very important part of parenting. What other steps do super parents take in order to make sure their children are raised gifted?
7. Is it possible to measure parental influences? Why or why not?

Suggested Readings

Campbell, James Reed. *Raising Your Child To Be Gifted: Successful Parents Speak!* Boston:
Brookline Books, 1995.
Harris, Judith Rich. *The Nurture Assumption: Why Children Turn Out The Way They Do*. New York: Simon & Schuster, 1998.
Rhodes, Celeste. "Modeling Interdependence: Productive Parenting For Gifted Adolescents." *Journal of Secondary Gifted Education* 5, no. 4 (April 1994): 19–26.

Webb, Meckstroth E., and Stephanie S. Tolan. *Guiding the Gifted Child: A Practical Source For Parents and Teachers*. Scottsdale, AZ: Gifted Psychology Press, 1994.

CHAPTER TWO   THE BRAIN:
A COMPLEX AND REMARKABLE ORGAN

Study Questions

Discussion: Why is it important for parents and educators to gain knowledge about the growth and function of the teenage brain? How might this knowledge be useful?

Suggested Readings

Hampden-Turner, Charles. *Maps of The Mind*. New York: Macmillan Publishing Company, 1982.
Rose, Colin. *Accelerated Learning*. New York: Dell Publishing, 1985.

CHAPTER THREE   DEFINING GIFTED AND TALENTED

Study Questions

1. What judgment may be concluded from the variety of definitions listed in the gifted and talented category?
2. Which definition of gifted and talented do you find relevant? Why?
3. What, in your opinion, is a final consideration that one must acknowledge when describing a gifted and talented individual?

Suggested Readings

Davis, Gary A., and Sylvia B. Rimm. *Education of The Gifted and Talented*. 4d ed. Needham Heights, MA: Allyn & Bacon, 1998.
Gardner, Harold. *Frames of Mind: The Theory of Multiple Intelligences*. New York: Basic Books, 1985.
Maker, C. J. "Identification of Gifted Minority Students: A National Problem, Needed Changes and a Promising Solution." *Gifted Child Quarterly* 40, no. 1 (January 1996): 41-50.
Marland, Sidney. "Education of The Gifted and Talented." Report to The Congress of the United States by the U.S. Commissioner of Education. Washington, D.C.: U.S. Government Printing Office, 1972.
Miller, Alice. *The Drama of The Gifted Child: The Search For The True Self*. New York: Perseus Books Group, 1997.

Renzulli, Joseph. "The Three-ring Conception of Giftedness: A Developmental Model for Creative Productivity. Pp. 53-92 in *Conceptions of Giftedness*, edited by R.J. Sternberg & J.E. Davidson. Cambridge, MA: Cambridge University Press, 1986.
Sternberg, Robert J. *The Triarchic Mind: A New Theory of Human Intelligence*. New York: Viking, 1988.

CHAPTER FOUR   ACHIEVEMENT

Study Questions

1. It has been stated that we all possess the motivation to achieve. Is this motivation inborn? Explain your answer.
2. Why is it important for children to possess self-esteem? How can parents raise their children's self-esteem?
3. From a philosophical or a moralistic point of view, what metaphor best symbolizes Maslow's suggestions about learning? Answers will vary.
4. There are people in our society today who cannot read or write, what causes illiteracy in a country that has public education? Why is illiteracy detrimental to our society?
5. How does social influence affect a child's academic achievement and, to a greater degree, our world.

Suggested Readings

Harris, Judith R. *The Nurture Assumption: Why Children Turn Out The Way They Do*. New York: Simon & Schuster, 1998.
Johnson, Eric W. *Raising Children to Achieve*. New York: Walker and Company, 1984.
Kozol, Jonathan. *Illiterate America*. New York: Anchor Press/Doubleday, 1985.
McLaren, Peter. *Life in Schools: An Introduction to Critical Pedagogy*. New York: Longman, 1994.
Maslow, Abraham H. *The Farther Reaches of Human Nature*. New York: Viking Press, 1971.
Mead, George H. *Mind, Self and Society*. Chicago: The University of Chicago Press, 1934.
Orenstein, Peggy. *Schoolgirls: Young Women, Self-esteem, and the Confidence Gap*. New York: Random House, 1994.

CHAPTER FIVE   FEMALES: A STORY FROM THE PAST

Study Question

1. What are the underlying causes of the inequality that confronted females two centuries ago . . . that confronts females today?

2. The struggle for equality for females is ongoing, in which major areas of our systems does this inequality affect females the most?
3. During the past 25 years, women have made measurable progress to gain equality, what more must women do to close the gap?

Suggested Readings

American Association of University Women. Pp 12-15 in *National Leadership Publication*, 1 February 1999.

Banner, Lois. *Elizabeth Cady Stanton*. New York: Little, Brown, 1980.

Friedan, Betty. *The Feminine Mystique*. New York: Norton, 1983.

Henry, Sherrye. *The Deep Divide*. New York: Macmillan, 1994.

National Coalition of Advocates for Students. *Barriers to Excellence: Our Children at Risk*. Boston: Author, 1985.

National Women's History Project. "History of The Movement." <http://www.legacy98.org/move-hist.html> (1998)

CHAPTER SIX   THE DILEMMA OF GIFTED AND TALENTED FEMALES

Study Questions

1. The words "underachieving gifted students" seem to be a contradiction; yet, several child psychologists have described these students' behavior. What factors contribute to the underachieving dilemma of gifted students?
2. How does our society contribute to the passive role of some females?
3. What are some of the reasons why gifted minority females are not identified as gifted?
4. Why is it important to identify gifted underachievers?

Suggested Readings

Dabrowski, Kazimierz. *Psychoneurosis Is Not An Illness*. London: Gryf, 1972.

Davis, Gary A., and Sylvia B. Rimm. *Education of Gifted and Talented*. 4d ed. Needham Heights, MA: Allyn & Bacon, 1998.

Ford, Donna. "Underachievement: An Investigation of the Paradox of Underachievement Among Gifted Black Students." *Roeper Review* 16, no. 2, (February 1993): 78–84.

Ford, Donna. *Reversing Underachievement Among Gifted Black Students: Promising Practices And Programs*. New York: Teachers College Press, 1996.

Kerr, Barbara. *Smart Girls: A New Psychology of Girls, Women and Giftedness*. Scottsdale, AZ: Gifted Psychology Press, 1994.

Noble, Kathleen. "Female and Gifted: The Challenge." *Gifted Unlimited.* Bellevue, WA: North West Gifted Child Association, 1988.

Rimm, Sylvia B. *Why Bright Kids Get Poor Grades.* New York: Crown Trade Paperbacks, 1995.

Webb, James, Elizabeth Meckstroth, and Stephanie Tolan. *Guiding the Gifted Child: A Practical Source For Parents and Teachers.* Scottsdale, AZ: Gifted Psychology Press, 1994.

Whitmore, Joanne R. *Giftedness, Conflict, and Underachievement.* Boston: Allyn & Bacon, 1980.

CHAPTER SEVEN   STAGING AN INTERVIEW WITH GIFTED AND TALENTED FEMALES

Study Questions

1. This qualitative-narrative study used an interview approach to record participants' stories about how parental influences helped them to achieve. How does this investigatory process lend credibility to an inquiry?
2. Why is it important to set the stage for an interview and to use structured guidelines during the formal interview process?

Suggested Readings

Buchanan, Nina, and John Feldhusen. *Conducting Research and Evaluation in Gifted Education: A Handbook of Methods and Applications.* (Patterns of Influence on Gifted Learners, Pp. 102-124). New York: Teachers College Press, 1991.

Lincoln, Yvonna, and Egon Guba. *Naturalistic Inquiry.* Newbury Park, CA.: Sage Publications, 1985.

CHAPTER EIGHT   GIFTED AND TALENTED FEMALES SPEAK OUT!

Study Questions

1. What was the significance of using the three human development staged to construct the "Open-ended" questions for the interview with the participants?
2. The participants conversed about how their parents influenced them to achieve. From whose perspective are the stories told?
3. What are some common themes that can be decoded from all of the participants' stories?
4. What did both the parents and their daughters value highly?
5. In which specific area did the participants show strong self-motivation?

Suggested Readings

Bingham, Mindy, and Sandy Stryker. *Things will be Different for my Daughter*. New York: Penguin Books, 1995.

Johnson, Eric W. *Raising Children to Achieve*. New York: Walker, 1984.

Rimm, Sylvia B. *How to Parent so Children will Learn*. New York: Three Rivers Press, 1996.

CHAPTER NINE   READING FOR ACHIEVEMENT

Study Questions

1. While narrating their stories, several participants made reference to reading. What are the implications that pertain to reading during early childhood?
2. Which participant became an avid reader due to an emotional crisis that occurred during her early childhood? Please explain your answer.
3. How did the community where the participants lived help them advance their skills in reading achievement?

Suggested Reading

Cochran-Smith, Marilyn. *The Making of a Reader*. New Jersey: Ablex Publishing Corporation, 1985.

CHAPTER TEN   DISCUSSION AND CONCLUSION

Study Questions

1. How does a child's success begin?
2. What does translating parental expectations mean?
3. How did the participants respond to their parents' encouragement?
4. How did the advice that was given by the parents to their daughters motivate them to achieve?
5. How did support help the participants grow and be successful?
6. All children must be nurtured; however, why is it extremely important to nurture female children, especially gifted females?

Suggested Readings

Bingham, Mindy, and Sandy Stryker. *Things will be Different for my Daughter*. New York: Penguin Books, 1995.

Campbell, James R. *Raising Your Child To Be Gifted: Successful Parents Speak!* Boston: Brookline Books, 1995.

Collins, Marva. *"Ordinary" Children, Extraordinary Teachers.* Hampton, VA: Hampton Roads, 1992.

Gardner, Harold. *Frames of Mind: The Theory of Multiple Intelligences.* New York: Basic Books, 1985.

Kerr, Barbara A. *Smart Girls: A New Psychology of Girls, Women and Giftedness.* Scottsdale, AZ: Gifted Psychology Press, 1994.

Rimm, Sylvia, Sara Rimm Kaufman, and Ilonna Rimm. *See Jane Win: The Rimm Report on How 1,000 Girls Became Successful Women.* New York: Crown Publishers, 1999.

Schmitz, Connie, and Judy Galbraith. *Managing the Social and Emotional Needs of the Gifted.* Minneapolis, MN: Free Spirit, 1985.

Appendix

Optimum Achievement Model

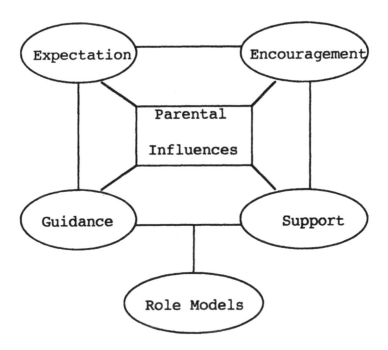

The 5 parental influences, pictured above in a design of connectivity, represent invaluable measures to obtain optimum achievement for all children, especially gifted and talented females.

Source: Mary Henderson
2005

Bibliography

American Association of University Women. Pp. 12-15 in *National Leadership Publication*, 1 February 1999.

Banner, Lois. *Elizabeth Cady Stanton*. New York: Little, Brown, 1980.

Bingham, Mindy, and Sandy Stryker. *Things will be Different for my Daughter*. New York: Penguin Books, 1995.

Buchanan, Nina, and John Feldhusen. *Conducting Research and Evaluation in Gifted Education A Handbook of Methods and Applications*. (Patterns of Influence on gifted Learners, Pp. 102-124). New York: Teachers College Press, 1991.

Campbell, James Reed. *Raising Your Child to be Gifted: Successful Parents Speak!* Boston: Brookline Books, 1995.

Cochran-Smith, Marilyn. *The Making of a Reader*. New Jersey: Ablex Publishing Corporation, 1985.

Collins, Marva. *"Ordinary" Children, Extraordinary Teachers*. Hampton, VA: Hampton Roads, 1992.

Dabrowski, Kazimierz. *Psychoneurosis Is Not An Illness*. Lond: Gryf, 1972.

Davis, Gary A., and Sylvia B. Rimm. *Education of Gifted and Talented*. 4d ed. Needham Heights, MA: Allyn & Bacon, 1998.

Ford, Donna. "Underachievement: An Investigation of the Paradox of Underachievement Among Gifted Black Students." *Roeper Review* 16, no. 2, (February 1993): 78-84.

Ford, Donna. *Reversing Underachievement Among Gifted Black Students: Promising Practices and Programs*. New York: Teachers College Press, 1996.

Friedan, Betty. *The Feminine Mystique*. New York: Norton, 1983.

Gardner, Harold. *Frames of Mind: The Theory of Multiple Intelligences*. New York: Basic Books, 1985.

Hampden-Turner, Charles. *Maps of The Mind*. New York: Macmillan Publishing Company, 1982.

Harris, Judith Rich. *The Nurture Assumption: Why Children Turn Out The Way They Do*. New York: Simon & Schuster, 1998.

Henderson, Mary. "Achievement: An Exploration of Parental Influences on Gifted and Talented Females from Culturally Diverse Backgrounds. Ed.D. diss., Fielding Graduate University, 2001. Abstract in *UMI Dissertation Services* (2002): 3032090.

Henry, Sherrye. *The Deep Divide*. New York: Macmillan, 1994.

Johnson, Eric W. *Raising Children to Achieve*. New York: Walker and Company, 1984.

Kerr, Barbara. *Smart Girls: A New Psychology of Girls, Women and Giftedness*. Scottsdale, AZ: Gifted Psychology Press, 1994.

Kozol, Jonathan. *Illiterate America*. New York: Anchor Press/Doubleday, 1985.

Lincoln, Yvonna, and Egon Guba. *Naturalistic Inquiry*. Newbury Park, CA: Sage Publications, 1985.

Maker, C.J. "Identification of Gifted Minority Students: A National Problem, Needed Changes
and a Promising Solution." *Gifted Child Quarterly* 40, no. 1 (January 1996): 41-50.

Marland, Sidney. "Education of the Gifted and Talented." Report to the Congress of the United States by the U.S. Commissioner of Education. Washington, D.C.: U.S. Government Printing Office, 1972.

Maslow, Abraham H. *The Farther Reaches of Human Nature*. New York: Viking Press, 1971.

McLaren, Peter. *Life in Schools: An Introduction to Critical Pedagogy*. New York: Longman, 1994.

Mead, George H. *Mind, Self and Society*. Chicago: The University of Chicago Press, 1934.

Miller, Alice. *The Drama of the Gifted Child: The Search for the True Self*. New York: Perseus Books Group, 1997.

National Coalition of Advocates for Students. *Barriers to Excellence: Our Children at Risk* Boston: Author, 1985.

National Institute of Mental Health. (February 11, 2005) <http://www.nimh.nih.gov/>

National Women's History Project. "History of The Movement." (1998) <http://www.legacy98.org/move-hist.html>

Noble, Kathleen. "Female and Gifted: The Challenge." *Gifted Unlimited*. Bellevue, WA: North West Gifted Child Association, 1988.

Orenstein, Peggy. *Schoolgirls: Young Women, Self-esteem, and the Confidence Gap*. New York: Random House, 1994.

Renzulli, Joseph. "The Three-ring Conception of Giftedness: A Developmental Model for Creative Productivity. Pp. 53-92 in *Conceptions of Giftedness*, edited by R. J. Sternberg & J. E. Davidson. Cambridge, MA: Cambridge University Press, 1986.

Rimm, Sylvia B. *How to Parent so Children will Learn*. New York: Three Rivers Press, 1996.

Rimm, Sylvia, Sara Rimm Kaufman, and Ilonna Rimm. *See Jane Win: The Rimm Report on How 1,000 Girls Became Successful Women*. New York: Crown Publishers, 1999.

Rhodes, Celeste. "Modeling Interdependence: Productive Parenting for Gifted Adolescents." *Journal of Secondary Gifted Education* 5, no. 4 (April 1994): 19-26.

Rose, Colin. *Accelerated Learning.* New York: Dell Publishing, 1985.

Schmitz, Connie, and Judy Galbraith. *Managing the Social and Emotional Needs of the Gifted.* Minneapolis, MN: Free Spirit, 1985.

Stankowski, W.M. "Definition." In *Simple Gifts*, edited by R. E. Clasen and B. Robinson. Madison: University of Wisconsin-Extension, 1978.

Sternberg, Robert J. *TheTtriarchic Mind: A New Theory of Human Intelligence.* New York: Viking, 1988. The Associated Press, 23 July 2004.

Thornborrow, Nancy, and Marianna Sheldon. "Women in the Labor Force." (2004). <http://www.dac.neu.edu/womens.studies/sheldon.htm>

Voice of The Times, 7 July 2004

Webb, James, Elizabeth Meckstroth, and Stephanie Tolan. *Guiding the Gifted Child: A Practical Source For Parents and Teachers.* Scottsdale, AZ: Gifted Psychology Press, 1994.

Whitmore, Joanne R. *Giftedness, Conflict, and Underachievement.* Boston: Allyn & Bacon, 1980.

Index

About the Author

Mary E. Henderson is a teacher with the Anchorage School District, Anchorage, Alaska. She is a 2001 graduate of Fielding Graduate University, Santa Barbara, California, where she earned a doctorate in Educational Leadership and Change. She has done extensive research on gifted and talented females, parental influences, and achievement. Her research has been presented at the American Educational Research Association Annual Meetings.

Lightning Source UK Ltd.
Milton Keynes UK
UKHW012228300520
364101UK00001B/22